michell

from

SURVIVING
to THRIVING

7 simple steps to help
you live a life you love!

a portion of the proceeds from this book will be donated
to support mental health initiatives worldwide

Published by: Profits Publishing

http://profitspublishing.com/

US Address
1300 Boblett Street, Unit A- 218
Blaine, WA, 98230
Phone: 866-492-6623
Fax: 250-493-6603

Canadian Address
1265 Charter Hill Drive
Coquitlam, BC, V3E 1P1
Phone: 604-941-3041
Fax: 604-944-7993

From Surviving to Thriving

7 Simple Steps to Help You Live a Life You LOVE!

ISBN: 978-1-933817-43-9

http://momentumworks.com

DEDICATION:

For Talia, the sunshine of my life

Table of Contents

Michelle Richardson

"What lies behind us and what lies before us are tiny matters compared to what lies within us."

Ralph Waldo Emerson

Acknowledgements

So many people have contributed to the creation of this book. Those of special note are my parents, Mack & Gail, who have always believed in me and instilled self-confidence and values which have fueled my accomplishments and enabled me to emerge through the ups and downs in my life an ever stronger, more authentic and compassionate person. My sisters, Debra Campbell & Carmen Disiewich, who provide lots of love, support, input and opportunities for me to discover and be who I am. My best friend Sandra Weiser, who contributed valuable feedback and ideas, and has been firmly behind me, beside me and on my team through thick and thin since kindergarten. Eric Weiser for his support, feedback and suggestions at various points along the way. My two godsons, nephew and niece who I love dearly and who provide abundant evidence that the future of humanity is in the hands of kind, considerate, adventurous and brilliant young people. The rest of my incredible family & friends, too numerous to mention. Maximum Velocity, the amazing team of people who are like family to me, for their feedback and for supporting me to play big games and have fun in the process (and always managing to assemble the most delicious array of appetizers for our monthly meetings). My clients, colleagues, mentors and Coach who have contributed to my life and experiences and, as a result, this book in meaningful ways. Bob Burnham, who provided me with a key to unlock the process of filling these pages; Gary Spencer-Smith & Brian Snee for sharing their ideas, which helped me put a few final pieces in place. Jodi Bepler for her assistance with formatting and many other publishing related activities.

Tim Bepler for capturing my vision for the cover so beautifully... you have an incredible gift. And finally, my husband Dan and daughter Talia... the ultimate inspiration for my completion of this book.

With love and heartfelt gratitude,

Michelle

"Be the change you wish to see in the world."

Gandhi

FOREWORD

In today's world where the pace seems to become more rapid by the day, people often take the back seat to duty and possessions, information is delivered at break-neck speed, and we struggle to keep up with it all. We usually end up at the back of our own bus. It would be easy to resign ourselves to the 'fact' that "that's just how life is these days" and continue on our current course. I am suggesting that there is a different way to approach life and that this approach leads to happiness and fulfillment, something that everyone I've ever met, whether in my personal life, through my coaching practice, or in business, says they want.

The 'fact' is that we have a choice as to how we will live our lives and how much or how little we will buy into what the world we live in is selling. It is fully within our power to decide how much we will take on, what is most important to us, and how we will spend our time and energy. In my experience only a small portion of the population really knows what is most important to them or how to go about figuring it out if they want to. We spend more time deciding what to wear than we do getting to know ourselves and deciding how to design our lives so that we thrive, rather than simply survive.

This book is intended to assist you in discovering more about who you are, what is important to you, what the elements of your best life are, and how to go about creating it. Its objective is to significantly increase your chances of experiencing happiness and fulfillment at a deep level so that you will jump out of bed each day excited about what lies ahead. The information, exercises and outcomes are designed to help you become clear about what that looks like for you. My hope is that you will create clarity, have more time and energy for what's most important, and your life will be richer and more fun as a result. This, in turn, will see your life impacted in a profoundly positive way.

Enjoy the journey…

Michelle

*"Your Vision will become clear only when you look into your heart. Who looks outside, dreams.
Who looks inside, awakens."*

Jung

AUTHOR'S NOTE

In my journey of personal discovery and evolution, I have had my share of triumphs and challenges. Through my experiences, extensive personal and professional development, and coaching thousands of people, I have learned a lot about happiness, success, fulfillment and what it takes to create these things. I've also learned that there is as much value in the challenges, perhaps even more so, as in the triumphs. I now have ways to pick myself up, dust myself off, and get back to what I know works to keep me thriving despite the circumstances in my life. This is what I wish for everyone and what I will share with you in this book. My hope is that it will help you thrive and better equip you for whatever lies ahead.

By investing about 30 minutes a day for 30 days you could go from Surviving to Thriving; assuming, of course, that you do the work and apply what you learn. In the process of navigating through this book you will be challenged to be honest with yourself, dedicate time and energy, answer questions that you may not have considered before, and make choices (not always easy ones) that will result in you living your best life. And by best life I mean the life that is best for you, the one that leads to happiness and fulfillment for YOU.

You will likely be enjoying more of what you want, or at least enjoying life more, well before you read the last page or complete the last exercise. You will also know how to sustain this in the long run, which is important if you are to reap the benefits for the rest of your life, which I hope you will. What good would this work be if its impact ended once you finish this book? Which reminds me to remind you to be compassionate with yourself; the changes won't happen overnight and it will likely take more than a few attempts to incorporate new things into your life… it is a lifelong journey.

May you always thrive and share what you've learned with others so that we all enjoy a life of happiness and fulfillment and live in a much happier world.

Thrive and be fully alive!

Michelle

How To Use This Book

This book is designed to be completed in 90 days or less; as much as the work is valuable when completed at any pace, momentum plays a role in its effectiveness. Delay has the propensity to reduce its effectiveness and the longevity of results. Not to mention that it takes a certain level of commitment, which I believe is imperative, to complete this work in 90 days or less. This book is also designed to be valuable whether you choose to complete the assignments or not.

- Each Chapter introduces a "Thriving Strategy" and includes background information and learning opportunities designed to help you understand the Thriving Strategy.

- Each Chapter includes "Momentum Work", an assignment designed to guide you through a self-discovery process, create momentum, and assist you in getting the Thriving Strategy working in your life.

- There is an "Ongoing Assignment" for each chapter, intended to help you integrate the Thriving Strategy into your daily life, which will help you realize long term results from this work.

- At the end of each chapter you will find ideas to support you in implementing each Thriving Strategy in your life. These ideas will be helpful when completing the Momentum Work and integrating the strategies long term.

Some suggested schedules for reading this book and completing the Momentum Work are found in the table below.

Chapter & Assignment	30 Day Schedule	Weekly Schedule	60 Day Schedule	90 Day Schedule
1	Day 1-4	Day 1-7	Day 1-8	Day 1-12
2	Day 5-8	Day 8-14	Day 9-16	Day 13-25
3	Day 9-13	Day 15-21	Day 17-25	Day 26-37
4	Day 14-17	Day 22-28	Day 26-34	Day 38-51
5	Day 18-21	Day 29-35	Day 35-43	Day 52-64
6	Day 22-25	Day 36-42	Day 44-52	Day 65-77
7	Day 26-30	Day 43-49	Day 53-60	Day 78-90

If you start reading this book and stop yourself from moving forward because of the assignments, read on anyway. Come back to the assignments later. They key is to get momentum going and start to incorporate what you learn as soon as possible. It can also be fun to engage a friend or group of people in the process of completing this book.

I have created a Companion Workbook to go along with this book; it is designed to help you move more quickly and effectively from Surviving to Thriving. Within its pages you will find all of the Momentum Work Assignments clearly laid out so that everything you learn, discover about yourself, and commit to do will be easily accessible in one place. It will also serve as a useful reference to help you keep the momentum going and enable you to gain maximum benefit from this book over time. The Ongoing Assignments for each chapter are also included.

The Companion Workbook is available for purchase in electronic format at http://momentumworks.com for $4.99.

Congratulations on your decision to move forward! In my experience, the voyage of self-discovery is always worthwhile and leads to a richer, more rewarding life… that is, after all, why we're here.

Enjoy the journey…

Michelle

*"The best way to predict your future
is to create it."*

Erich Fromm

Thriving Strategy #1
Take Charge

Take Charge - Defined

Taking Charge is about getting into the driver's seat of your life and taking it where YOU want it to go. Its foundation is based on ownership, empowerment and ability. It requires a willingness to look honestly and objectively at yourself and your results and become conscious about what is working and what is not. It's the "if it is to be (or not to be) it is up to me" in life. It involves being willing to look at what it is about you that contributes to your results, both those you like and those you don't like. Taking Charge means owning all of it... and knowing that you have the power and choice to change or continue with whatever you want.

Personal Responsibility

The essence of Personal Responsibility is that you create your results, whether you like them or not, and if you want things to be different it is up to you to make them so. This is not a revolutionary new concept, it is one that has long proven to be very effective in generating desired results. In a sense it's the "I can" vs. "I can't". It may sound simple in theory, but in practice it generally proves not to be so. We often prefer to take responsibility for the things we like and blame people and/or circumstances for the things we don't. If only 'they' would change, if only 'they' did/didn't do this, if only this did/didn't happen. Personal Responsibility is the foundation upon which absolutely fabulous lives are built; without it, the best laid plans have the potential to crumble around you.

Advantages of Taking Charge

There are many compelling reasons to Take Charge of your life, rather than blame other people and/or circumstances for why your life isn't the way you want it be. Among them are that it is a very powerful and action-oriented place to live from. Once you decide to adopt this approach, it is about taking your life into your own hands and creating what you want. From this place you increase the likelihood of having the life you envision, one you really want. Your energy turns toward the 'hows' and 'whats' of your life and away from the 'whys'. You take more action, which increases your self-esteem and self-confidence and gets you where you want to go faster. By focusing on what you want, you will get more of it and this leads to a life you love.

Differences to Expect in Your Life

Generally, when you Take Charge your life works better. You tend to attract different people and situations into your life when you come from a place of ownership. You enjoy life more and tend to take life less seriously, rolling with the ups and downs more easily. You also generate better results in terms of what is most important to you. Your relationships improve as you move away from blaming others and look at how you contribute to all of the outcomes in your life. You have more faith in yourself and your ability to create what you want. The more you Take Charge, the more you want to Take Charge and the more satisfied you become with your life as it is. You experience increased confidence, joy and fulfillment.

Consequences of Relinquishing Responsibility

When you let life 'happen' to you, you tend to have a less than rewarding experience of it. Precious time and energy are wasted on things that are outside of your control. You may even become bitter, resentful, or angry at the course your life has taken or the events that have occurred. This negatively impacts your relationship with yourself as well as the people in your life. You tend to attract people of similar mind, which keeps you stuck in a negative place. You most certainly will not fulfill your life's purpose in a meaningful way, if at all. Your life will likely have a perpetual undercurrent of dissatisfaction.

25

Taking Charge and Relationships

Taking Charge can have a very positive impact on your relationships. When you take a position of ownership in your life, you have a stronger sense of self and of your ability to create what you want. You also have the belief that you deserve it. You become more independent, confident, decisive and clear and therefore come to relationships from a place of strength and abundance rather than 'needing' something from someone else. From this place you are less likely to 'pass the buck' to someone else when things don't go as you want them to. You also have a keen sense of being in control of your life as opposed to being at the mercy of the events that occur.

What to Take Charge Of

Taking Charge refers to taking ownership of all aspects of your life. This includes yourself, your actions, your results (whether you like them or not), your relationships, your happiness... literally everything. By taking this position you are empowered to make whatever changes you deem appropriate given the gap between what you want and what you have (your results). As much as it may seem somewhat scary to take ownership of ALL of your life, it can also be very liberating and have many big benefits. When you decide "if it is to be, it's up to me" you will realize that you can do, be and have whatever you want and then set about creating it.

The Power in Taking Charge

The power in Taking Charge lies squarely with you. This is among the biggest benefits of adopting this approach to life. When you cease to believe that other people, circumstances, situations, etc. have the power to determine your results, you tend to take action from a very powerful place. Henry Ford said "Whether you think you can or can't, you're right." This really speaks to the idea that the power lies within you to do whatever you want to do. If you think of this in terms of driving a car vs. being a passenger... the driver has the power. By taking a position of ownership, you take the wheel in your life and become the driver.

Resistance in Relationships

Sometimes people in your life aren't as excited as you are about the changes you make. People are used to you being a certain way and when you are different it can change the dynamics of a relationship, especially if someone in your life feels threatened in some way by the changes they see. For example, if you to tend be a helper and you decide that you're going to Take Charge of your life and leave others to do the same, the people you used to help might not like this change. It can be useful to share the changes you are making with the important people in your life in the spirit of including them and potentially gaining their support. Having said that, their approval and support are not necessary... these things are outside of your control and have the potential to take you off

27

track if you allow them to. As long as you are clear about why you're adopting this position and remain committed to yourself, the benefits will likely outweigh any pushback you might experience from others.

How Taking Charge Helps You Thrive

Taking Charge helps you thrive by empowering you to affect and direct the course of your life. Rather than looking for reasons why your life is the way it is or isn't the way you want it to be, you take action to move things closer to what you want. You make the changes required and have the tools necessary to help you enjoy the journey more. Rather than thinking you have to wait until some future date or event occurs in order to be happy, you can choose happiness in any and every moment along the way. When you Take Charge, you get where you want to go more quickly, you enjoy where you are more thoroughly, and you attract more people of like mind.

Take Charge: Key Concepts

- own all of your results
- a powerful, action-oriented place to live from
- take action from a place of ability
- creates stronger relationships (with yourself and others)
- focus on 'hows' and 'whats' rather than 'whys'

Momentum Work

1. Go to http://momentumworks.com/resources.html. Download and complete the Personal Assessment, then complete the rest of this assignment.

   a. The area(s) of my life that are working best are:

   b. The area(s) of my life that are working least well are:

2. What I am doing (or not doing) in the areas that are working best that could help me get more of what I want in the areas that are working least well is:

3. Choose one area of your life that you want to improve your results in.

   a. Identify 3 things you will do within the next 7 days to improve this area
   b. Complete those 3 things within 7 days
   c. Reward yourself as you complete each item on your list

29

Ongoing Assignment:

Take Charge of your life for the duration of this book, and beyond if you think it is useful. Celebrate your successes along the way.

Ideas About Taking Charge:

1. Identify the areas of your life that you hear yourself complaining about often; this indicates an area that you are clearly not Taking Charge of (ask your family/friends for help as well)

2. Think about what you consider to be the worst thing that has happened in your life and write down as many positive outcomes about it as possible (ask for help if you want it)

3. Write down all of the things you tell yourself as to why you don't have what you want in your life now and write out at least one counter argument for each one; take action in the direction of what you want from a place of why you can vs. why you tell yourself you can't

4. Remind yourself that everything in life is a choice and choose to Take Charge rather than fall victim to people/ events/situations in your life

"The real voyage of discovery consists not in seeking new landscapes, but in having new eyes."

Marcel Proust

Thriving Strategy #2
Be Grateful

Be Grateful - Defined

Being Grateful is all about recognizing and appreciating the good that already exists in your life; it is one of the quickest and easiest ways to enjoy life more. This applies to big and small things and it requires daily, if not more frequent, attention. The Law of Concentration states that "what you focus on expands in your experience". The basis of the Law of Attraction is that you get whatever you give your time, attention and energy to, whether wanted or unwanted. Taken individually or combined, the message is that if you focus on the good things in your life, you will experience more good things. Conversely, if you focus on what's not good in your life, you will get more of those things. Further, until you appreciate what you have, it is unlikely that you will get more. There are many things for which you may be grateful, including your family, positive experiences you have, your health, personal qualities, beautiful things you observe, things that make your life easier, lessons you learn, the kindness of a stranger or someone you know, and serendipity or 'coincidences', to name a few. Once you start to focus on what's right about your life, your experience of life will improve significantly and you will begin to get more of what you want.

Advantages of Being Grateful

There are many advantages to having an attitude of gratitude, some of the biggest being that your outlook on life is more positive and your overall experience is more joyful. When you start to pay attention to all that is good, you will notice and get more of it. The shift in energy that comes with noticing and appreciating all that is good in your life effects change in every area of your life. The more you notice and are grateful for what you have, the more good comes to you. It is very much a matter of being more aware of and intentional about the things you are grateful for. When you choose an attitude of gratitude your life flows better, things come more readily and easily, and you experience more happiness as a result. Appreciating the big and small, tangible and intangible, living and inert, and serendipitous and intentional, builds a strong foundation for a life you love.

Hardships and Gratitude

In situations of hardship, whether long-standing or sporadic, it can be helpful to start by looking for small things to be grateful for. It is possible, in fact it's highly likely, that by focusing on the hardship you are getting more of the same. To begin to put an end to this cycle, focus on what is good (i.e., do you have a great friend, a favorite chair, a soft blanket, is there something you appreciate in nature, a place that you feel safe?). Eventually, as you practice this, you will notice more good and at some point you may even find the good in the hardships you've experienced. It often requires some distance in your rearview mirror to truly appreciate the value of challenges in your life. Sometimes they are among the best teachers, testing grounds and catalysts for positive change.

For Those Not Grateful

If you're not grateful, chances are you're focusing on what you don't want and getting more of it. This is not to suggest that there aren't people who have experienced hardship or endured difficult times... most people have. It is to put forward that no matter how difficult or undesirable your current situation might seem, there is always something to be grateful for. Sometimes it's as fundamental as making it through a day, or being in good health, or having someone in your life that you really care about. Other times it is about reaching a particular milestone, experiencing good fortune, or having things go your way with ease. Most, if not all, people have faced challenges along the way but those who decide to look at them through a lens of gratitude have a better outlook on life. By taking steps toward being more grateful and understanding why you are not grateful, you will begin to swing the pendulum of your life in the direction you want it to go. This will have a significantly positive impact on your outlook and experience of life.

Gratitude is a Choice

Everything in your life is a choice... including gratitude. Not only is gratitude a choice, it is something that can be learned. Simply raising your awareness of and focusing on this concept is an excellent place to start. In pretty much every minute of every day you are faced with choices. Even situations and outcomes that you deem to be unfavorable can provide opportunities to be grateful. Sometimes the most challenging times in our life bring with them the greatest opportunities for growth and learning. It may take time to look back and reflect on these events from a place of gratitude, but not necessarily. In many instances unexpected or unwelcome endings eventually lead to better, more exciting beginnings. By choosing to look for a place from which to be grateful in all of the events of your life, you will create an environment in which more good naturally occurs.

The Relationship Between Gratitude and Luck

If thoughts and beliefs determine luck, gratitude is one very effective way to considerably impact your luck. Once you start to pay attention to everything you have to be grateful for, you begin to expect things to go the way you want them to... and they generally do. Your beliefs set the stage for your reality and so you attract more of what you want in your life. When you appreciate all of the experiences, circumstances, people, things, etc. that are present in your life, virtually everything becomes something to be grateful for and appreciate. At this point, it all becomes good fortune and your perspective shifts, which in turn shifts your life in a positive and empowered direction.

The Relationship Between Gratitude and Money

In as much as you are grateful for what you have, there is a relationship between gratitude and money. In as much as you are grateful for ALL that exists in your life your propensity to generate wealth, monetary and otherwise, increases. Certainly if you are experiencing financial stress, it can negatively impact your enjoyment of life... but it doesn't necessarily have to. It is often easier to be grateful in the absence of financial stress, but this is not always the case. This is evident in the many examples of people who have 'little' being happy and grateful, and people who have 'a lot' being unhappy and taking things for granted. Being grateful regardless of your financial situation requires conscious effort and ongoing focus; over time it becomes a way of being. Whether the money or gratitude comes first really depends on the person, their circumstances, and their outlook on life. Having money and possessions doesn't necessarily result in gratitude. Consciousness and choice do.

The Relationship Between Gratitude and Perspective

When it comes to gratitude, perspective is everything – and it can change everything. Whether the glass is half full or half empty depends on your perspective. Hindsight often provides a different perspective. The key is to find what there is to be grateful for in the moment, or at least as quickly thereafter as possible. Sometimes we take things for granted and don't realize that they are actually things to be grateful for. Often a person must lose something in order to truly appreciate it. With loss comes a change in perspective and often a newfound appreciation for what they had. Changing your perspective rather than wishing things were different can lead to happiness and fulfillment.

Why Gratitude is not Universal

Many people have not been exposed to the notion of gratitude in the sense that it is referred to here and are simply not aware of it as a framework for living. Also, given the pace most people keep these days, they are so busy working to achieve the next milestone or get to the next place that they don't stop long enough to realize everything they have to be grateful for. Generally, when something has always been present in your life (i.e., good health, family, money, etc.) you are more likely to take it for granted. Many of the messages that are delivered via various sources (i.e., family, media, teachers, etc.) focus on achieving material success. The message is more, better, faster; acquiring more, living up to certain expectations, achieving things quickly, etc. As such, people are so busy 'doing' that they don't take the time to notice all that they do have – material or otherwise.

How Being Grateful Helps You Thrive

When you appreciate all that you have, your outlook is more positive, you enjoy your life more, and you are more fun to be with. This energy tends to attract more of what you want and it helps you get through some of the inevitable challenges you will face along the way. Although the concept of 'like attracts like' is not a new one, it is rarely more evident than in the realm of gratitude. This is a framework from which evidence abounds and your belief strengthens around your ability to do, be and have whatever you want. When you truly appreciate what you have, you send a message to the universe that you are ready for more. The universe then responds by giving you more. Life can be a very rich and fulfilling journey when you appreciate what you have and receive more of what you really want.

Be Grateful: Key Concepts

- appreciate what you have; big and small
- incorporate daily (at a minimum)
- you will attract more of what you want
- share with others

Momentum Work

1. Make a list of 20 things you are grateful for.

2. Buy a journal that is pleasing to you (or use one that you have) and use it as your Gratitude Journal; write at least 5 entries into it daily. Some things you may want to include are:

   · What am I appreciative of or grateful for today?
   · What qualities do I appreciate about myself today or in general?
   · What do I appreciate about the important people in my life?
   · What seemed to 'flow' for me today?

3. Make a list of at least 3 ways (other than a Gratitude Journal) you will incorporate gratitude into your life. Choose one and do it this week.

Ongoing Assignment:

Maintain a gratitude consciousness throughout each day and be mindful of all that you have to be grateful for. Continue with your Gratitude Journal for the remainder of this book (and beyond if you find it to be beneficial).

Ideas About Being Grateful:

1. More ideas for your Gratitude Journal:

- What do I take for granted that I am grateful for?
- What feelings did I experience today?
- If I am grateful for something that someone else did or said, did I thank them?

41

2. Catch yourself and other people doing things 'right' and say so in the moment

3. Carry something tangible with you (a photo, small angel charm, shell, stone, etc.) at all times that reminds you to be grateful

4. Be mindful... live in the present so that you notice all that you have to be grateful for each and every day

5. Ask other people what they are grateful for, it will spread joy and possibly give you some ideas of things that you can add to your gratitude list

"And in the end it's not the years in your life that count, it's the life in your years."

Abraham Lincoln

Thriving Strategy #3
Include Play

Include Play - Defined

Include Play means to do things that bring you joy on a regular basis. These are the fun, obligation-free things that are often put on the back burner in favor of 'more important' things. Play is an important part of a life well loved; it can be a solo experience, or include others. It involves trying new things, experimenting and discovering a variety of things that bring you pleasure. Ideally you would Include Play each day and incorporate it into your daily routine. Things that bring you into the flow, make you laugh, and take you and your mind away from the responsibilities of life all qualify as Play. Play is about doing something simply for the joy of it. It's about increasing the 'fun factor' in your life, engaging in things that you are passionate about, and taking life less seriously. As we 'grow up' there seems to be little or no time to Include Play. With so many responsibilities and so much information to process, Play often falls by the wayside. I imagine that some of the happiest memories you have involve Play, yet it seems to come last on most priority lists. Perhaps there is a perceived lack of importance, it doesn't seem to be a responsible thing to do, or you have lost touch with what is fun for you. Whatever the reason, Including Play is an important part of a life in which you thrive.

The Experiences Associated with Play

There are many experiences associated with Play; among them are flow, lightness, fun, joy and passion. It is possible to have this experience in every area of your life. Many people do not design their lives in a way that they experience these things often enough. There is no stress associated with Play. Generally you will be in a state of flow, focused solely on what you are doing at that time and not thinking about any of the other things that are happening in your life. When you are at Play, you are living in the moment and enjoying it thoroughly. You will also experience a connectedness... to yourself, your environment and anyone else involved in Play with you. You can create the experiences associated with Play whenever you want, wherever you are... and it needn't cost any money. By incorporating more Play into your life you will have a much more positive experience and feel better about yourself. Including Play is one of the fastest and easiest ways to shift your energy and live a life you love.

Some Benefits of Including Play

There are so many benefits associated with Including Play and they tend to spill over into all areas of your life. When your life Includes Play your level of stress is reduced, you are more relaxed, and you have more fun. All of this means that you'll be enjoying life immensely. As you move forward, your outlook on life will improve and you'll notice more positive things occurring because you'll be attracting them through your actions and energy. Your relationships will also improve as you start to feel better about yourself and your life. You will likely include other people in some of your Play activities, which means more and better quality time with the important people in your life. As you try new and different things, you will be more stimulated and engaged. Play offers BIG benefits that you will reap once you make it a priority.

Including Play in a Busy Schedule

If you're like a lot of people, being too busy is one of the most common excuses for pretty much everything you don't do in your life that you'd like to do. The question is "What are you busy doing?" When you start to look at how you spend your time and what is most important, you will likely discover some things that you can cut out in order to create time to Play. Because many people consider Play to be an extravagance, something to indulge in when they have time, it is often absent from their life. In fact, Play is a critical component of living a life you love; it is not an option. Play is one of the best ways to recharge; it gives you energy that fuels every other area of your life. By making Play a low priority, you do the rest of your life a disservice. You will not be in a position to perform optimally if you don't make time for things you enjoy, are passionate about, that help you relieve stress, and are fun for you. Play is not an afterthought in living your best life, it is an integral part of a well designed life in which you thrive. Be very intentional about how you spend your time and it will become easier to Include Play in your busy schedule.

The Optimal Amount of Play

Everyone has a different 'ideal' where Play is concerned. The bottom line is that it is important to include as much Play as required in order for you function optimally and effectively in all areas of your life. At a minimum you will want to Include Play daily. Your target is to have the energy for everything you want to do, enjoy your whole life, and have reserves to draw on for the inevitable challenges along the way. You will know that you are including enough Play when you are mentally alert, positive, energetic, happy, living in the present, and at peace the majority of the time. If any of these pieces are missing, it's probably time to include more Play in your life. It is one of the quickest and most enjoyable ways to shift your experience of life in a positive direction. Check in with yourself at least daily to ensure that you are making Play the priority it deserves to be and dedicating the time required in order to thrive.

Include Play for Life

Although Play may look different at different times in your life, you never outgrow it. In fact, revisiting the Play of your childhood, youth, early adulthood and other phases of your life can be very effective in terms of helping you connect, or reconnect, with the experiences you associate with Play. You never outgrow the need for the lightness, fun, joy and passion associated with Play. The further you travel along the road of life, the higher the likelihood that Play will become a distant image in your rearview mirror. In the process you will leave a key element of a rich, joyful, fulfilling life behind. As you get older and your responsibilities increase, Including Play in your life will require that you be conscious and intentional. Once you have discovered, or rediscovered, the many benefits of Play you will be more inclined to make it a priority and realize how important it is regardless of your age.

The Relationship Between Play and Learning

Play and learning are close cousins. Through the act of Play there can exist an abundance of learning. Whether it is a new skill, idea, perspective or insight, learning opportunities abound through Play. Play brings greater levity and passion to life and the learning process. It can challenge you to do, be and think differently, expand your experiences, and take you places you never imagined. It can expose you to new horizons and enhance your creativity. You may even discover that (gasp!) you need not be good at something in order to enjoy it! As much as Play and learning are related, it is not necessary to learn in order to Play. You can use Play as a means of experiencing success and challenge yourself to try new things, get out of your comfort zone, and learn more about

49

what you require in order to have more fun, joy and passion in your life. Playing for Playing's sake is an important part of the equation. Including Play will see you living more of your life in a state of flow, living in the moment, and loving it!

Distinguishing Between Work and Play

There is a definite difference between work and Play. Having a job you love, one that doesn't feel like work, doesn't necessarily equate to Play. Play is something you engage in for the purpose of having fun and unplugging from your responsibilities for a time. If your work feels like Play that's terrific, but it's still important to incorporate some Play into your life each day. One true gauge of work vs. Play is your intuition, that inner knowing of the difference between when you are enjoying what you are doing and when you are Playing. Doing something for the joy of it is very different than doing something you enjoy. If there is a lightness, whimsy, frivolity to it, even better. Feeling unselfconscious and being fully engaged and present in the moment are some other good barometers that indicate whether you are at work or Play. As important as it is to do something you love for a living, Including Play is as important for living a life you love.

Committing to Include Play

If the idea of Play is a distant memory or you're simply not convinced that it will deliver any significant value, the best way to get behind it is to give it a try. It's not necessary to make a long term commitment to it in order to determine its value to you. If you begin by choosing to Include Play in your life as you read and work through this book, you will most certainly experience the multitude of benefits associated with Play. Even choosing to Play once will expose you to the benefits. It is through the experience that you will realize how important it is and decide to make it a priority. Commitments generally work like this: you imagine an experience(s) you will have as a result of doing something, you do that thing and realize the experience(s) you imagined, it then becomes a priority and over time your level of commitment to doing it increases until you ultimately incorporate it into your life.

Imagined ⇨ Realized ⇨ Priority ⇨ Commitment
Experience   Experience

If you add this to what you will discover in Chapter 4 and tie how Including Play helps you Experience Success, it will become a priority more quickly and you will be more committed to it sooner. As you shift toward Play as a priority rather than an afterthought and make a commitment to incorporate it into your life every day, it will become a part of your best life that you are unwilling to omit.

How Including Play Helps You Thrive

Including Play helps you thrive in so many ways and at so many levels. The act of Play brings positive emotions and experiences while contributing to your enjoyment of life. When you are experimenting, learning and growing, your mind is engaged in important activities. You will enjoy better physical, mental and emotional health as a result of Playing more. Your self-awareness, confidence and self-esteem will increase and you will broaden your life skills. You will enjoy stronger and closer connections with people and as a result your relationships will improve. Among the most important determinants of happiness and fulfillment is the quality of your relationships... with yourself and others. Including Play is one of the best ways to enhance these relationships and it is one of the most important things you can do to thrive.

Play: Key Concepts

- engage in things you are passionate about
- aim for fun, joy, flow, whimsy
- try new things
- by yourself and with others

Momentum Work

1. Write down 20 things that you would want to do that fall into the category of Play. Be sure to include at least 10 things you could do by yourself and 5 you could do with others.

    · Identify the Top 5 Play activities you would like to engage in

2. Write down all of the ways you spend your time. Prioritize them as follows:

    1 = important, something you spend enough time doing
    2 = important, something you'd like to spend more time doing
    3 = not important, time waster, distraction, or something you could eliminate

3. Look at the Priority 2 and 3 items on your list

    a. choose one Priority 3 item that you will eliminate
    b. add at least one Play activity (15 minutes or more) each day
    c. choose one Priority 2 item to make into a Priority 1 item by spending the additional time necessary for you to consider that you are spending enough time doing it

4. Choose one Play activity from your list that you have never done before and could do this week. Do it.

Ongoing Assignment:

Repeat Step 3 every week for the duration of this book. Ideally you will repeat this step until you are satisfied with the number of Priority 3 items and your Priority 2 items are given enough time to be considered Priority 1. Continue to add Play time, both solo and with others, into your life until you consider it to be the optimal amount for you.

Ideas About Including Play:

1. Continue to add to your list of activities that meet the criteria for Play. Consider:

   a. fun things you have enjoyed doing in the past that brought you joy

   b. times when you are/have been in flow

   c. things you are passionate about

d. things that children do at Play

e. things you think would be fun but haven't tried, or perhaps are somewhat afraid to try

2. Ask other people what they do for fun; add things you think you would enjoy to your list.

3. Examples of Play to get you started:

- Play a sport
- Play an instrument
- Go for a walk
- Color
- Paint
- Read
- Visit a winery
- Go bowling

- Run through a sprinkler
- Play a board game
- Take a fun class
- Toss or kick a ball with someone
- Sing
- Play with a dog
- Throw a frisbee
- Visit a bead store and make a piece of jewelry
- Fly a kite
- Play at a playground
- Do something fun with a child
- Go to a concert
- Build a sand castle
- Have a picnic
- Draw
- Go hiking
- Visit a local attraction
- Go swimming

"The best and most beautiful things in the world cannot be seen or touched, but are felt in the heart."

Helen Keller

Thriving Strategy #4
Experience Success

Experience Success - Defined

Experience Success means to learn what drives you and sustains you in the absence of everything else. This refers to your Personal Needs and Values. Personal Needs are those just above basic survival needs and they are among the most important elements of feeling successful every day. It may or may not surprise you that every person has a unique set of Personal Needs and that they are imperative if a person is to feel truly successful and happy. Values are defined as the things that are most important to us, ideals that we stand for in life. If you are not aligned with your Values, the experience of success will escape you. In our world, success is often defined in material terms; this is not what I am referring to. Although material success can certainly enhance your enjoyment of life, in itself it does not create an experience of success. The success to which I am referring doesn't require money, therefore anyone from any walk of life can create it. I am referring to the experiences that you require on a daily basis to feel vibrant and fully alive. What does this look like? Feel like? The result is feeling successful regardless of whether or not things turn out as you planned. It is about finding joy in the attempt, the process, the pursuit of your goals and dreams. With this knowledge and from this place you can Experience Success any time and any where.

Identifying Your Personal Needs

When identifying your Personal Needs, you must connect with the experiences in your life in which you felt happiest and most successful. Success is a feeling, a set of experiences that you can create for yourself in any given moment. In order to raise your awareness around your Personal Needs, be mindful of how you feel as you move through each day's events. Notice when you are doing something that generates a feeling of success, when you are enjoying something to the point that you lose track of time, when you experience pure happiness or joy, when you are unselfconsious. These are great indicators of meeting your Personal Needs. It is not a great relationship that contributes to your happiness, it is the experiences you have within the relationship that creates the feeling of happiness. It is not having the convertible that is attractive, it is the experience you imagine you will have when driving the convertible that you are ultimately after. It can also be useful to identify the patterns and actions you take that do not result in the outcomes you say you want. What are you struggling for or against? What outcomes are you generating that are undesirable? Whether you realize it or not, you get something you need out of everything you do. The question becomes whether or not it is helping you get what you want. Once you identify your Personal Needs you will be in a position to design your life to incorporate these all important elements and live life in a way that really works for you to Experience Success every day.

Identifying Your Values

Your attitude and approach to life are informed by your Values; they are the things that are most important to you. Your Values are based on choice, faith and who you are as a person. They encompass what you stand for and what you stand up for in life. Your Values gratify and attract you; you are naturally drawn to them. When you are engaged in something that goes against your Values, you will strongly resist it and possibly refuse to continue with it. If the idea that 'it goes against what I stand for/believe in' comes into play, it is a Values issue. When you live in alignment with your Values you will have a sense of meaning and fulfillment. Fulfillment is an outcome that most people desire and it is present when you thrive. By identifying your Values and living in alignment with them, you will have taken important steps toward living your best life.

Knowing When You Have Achieved Success

Once you determine your Personal Needs and Values, begin to incorporate them into your life, and feel more successful, you will develop a sense about it. As you get to know yourself better it will matter less what society or anyone other than you thinks success is. You will be more comfortable with and confident in yourself and happier with your life. You will more consciously and, ultimately, naturally choose to meet your Needs in ways that work for you to feel successful, notice when you are choosing strategies that aren't working, and course correct sooner. You will make choices and live your life according to what's most important to you. Your actions will directly relate to your Values and stated priorities and you will spend time on the things that really matter to you. You will experience more joy, more flow and less struggle in your life. Your work, personal life, relationships and everything else will work better and flow more easily. You will choose the smooth path rather than the bumpy one; you will listen to and trust your intuition to guide you in your choices and know when 'enough is enough'. You will be kind to yourself, compassionate, complimentary. You will experience a general sense of all being well in your world. You will know.

Experience More Success in Your Life

You can begin to experience more success in your life by planning your life to include people, activities and goals that meet your Personal Needs and align with your Values. Start small to build your confidence and experiment; be willing to try new things in the process. Break bigger things into more manageable pieces so that you enjoy 'wins' along the way. If, for example, you have determined that Challenge is one of your Personal Needs, you could set a challenging goal with milestones that are challenging but not overwhelming. By doing this you will feel successful every step of the way. Another important thing to do is to commit only to things that are important enough for you to actually follow through on. Do what you say you will do. This will not only help you align with your Values, it will also generate a feeling of success, and it is a real self-esteem booster. If you say 'yes' when you want to say 'no' and then don't do what you say you will do, the short term feeling of success you have when you make the commitment will be at the expense of a long term feeling of success and enhanced self-esteem. This is also and perhaps especially true for the commitments you make to yourself. When you renege on commitments to yourself, you may think that since only you know, it is less important. It is precisely because you know that it is even more important to do what you say you will do for yourself. Incorporating your Personal Needs and Values, and doing what you say you will do are some great ways to experience more success more often while enhancing your self-esteem.

Separating Yourself from Your Results

The idea that your results define or determine who you are at your core is a commonly held belief. It is also self-defeating. If you define yourself solely by your results, you will position yourself to be at the mercy of things outside of your control. If you have ever set out on a course that didn't end up as you imagined it would and made the leap to 'that was a flop and therefore I am a flop' you have done yourself a great disservice. At a minimum you have negatively affected your self-confidence and self-esteem; quite possibly you have allowed it to stop you from pursuing your dreams. Separating yourself from your results is very different than not taking ownership of your results. You can 'own' the fact that something didn't turn out as you had hoped and that you contributed to that result while acknowledging that you are not 'bad' or 'a failure' because of it. There is always something to be learned and there are always wins, even when things don't turn out the way you want them to. By looking for those things, you will Experience Success and recognize your intrinsic value. Once you understand that it is not your results that define you, but the qualities that prompted you to pursue a path in the first place, you can meet and/or overcome whatever challenges you may encounter. This is a powerful and self-honoring place to live your life from and pursue what you want most.

Feel Successful Regardless of the Outcome

Your expectations are what often set you up for disappointment or 'failure', so it is important to let go of expectations. In order to release expectations you must reframe your thought process, view outcomes as desires vs. expectations, and take action in the direction of what you desire. It is in the actions you take, not necessarily the final outcome, that success resides. Regardless of whether or not the end result is what you thought or hoped it would be, there will have been many successes along the way if you stop to reflect on the journey or better yet, stop and celebrate along the way. At a bare minimum there will have been the courage to take action, valuable learning, milestones to celebrate, and experiences of success imperative to your sense of fulfillment. When you choose to focus on these things rather than how things didn't work out as you had hoped, you will feel successful not only in the final result, but in the pursuit of something important as well as the steps in the journey.

A Void Despite Abundance

If you are someone who has everything you always thought you wanted and yet you have a sense that something is missing, there probably is. If you have gone about life in pursuit of things that you thought would result in happiness, it is possible that you have lost yourSELF along the way. Perhaps you followed that age-old map - finish school, go to college, get a job, get married, buy a house, have a family - without as much as a second thought... until now. Sure, you're happy enough, maybe you even have more than most, but isn't there something more to life? The answer to this question is a resounding 'YES', but have you stopped long enough to figure out what that is for YOU? What is missing may be any number of things but it quite likely centres around meaning, purpose, fulfillment, passion or something along those lines. External material success is terrific... it provides choice, freedom and peace of mind; in and of itself however, it does not bring happiness or fulfillment. These outcomes are a result of internal work... they are 'inside jobs', if you will. Getting to know who you really are and what is most important to you, and aligning your life with those things will likely fill the void you are feeling. When you do this, you will experience internal and external success, enjoy your life much more, and have more meaning in it.

Success Does Not Mean the Best

There are many factors that come into play where success is concerned. Certainly doing your best and striving for excellence are a couple of them, but being the best is not necessary. If it were, that would mean that there is room for only one person to be successful at any given thing. It would also mean that their success would be fleeting because the moment someone 'better' came along they would no longer be the best and by virtue of this fact, they would no longer be successful. That's simply not true. If you look at success in terms of your internal experience vs. some external expectation or measure, then you know that it is not about being the best. It is about designing your life in such a way that you generate a feeling of success by living your best life, that is, the life that's best for YOU. There is a vast difference between being the best and doing your best… which is really about playing to win. Understanding what playing to win looks like for you in all areas of your life is of paramount importance in creating experiences of success on an ongoing basis. Recognizing that your best may look different on any given day will also help. Holding the belief that everyone does their best at all times is a valuable position to take. When you realize that it is not necessary to be the best in order to be successful, you will cease to be concerned with what anyone other than you deems to be success. As a result, you will live a much more meaningful, authentic and enjoyable life.

Thriving and the Pursuit of Material Success

In and of itself, striving for material success is not a problem; it becomes a problem when you use it as a means of defining yourself and your worth. Material success can help make life easier and more enjoyable. It can also result in having many more options available to you. It is not, however, a guarantee for a rich, fulfilling life in which you are thriving. Viewing money or material wealth as a path to happiness can be very problematic. It relies on the occurrence of some future event in order for you to be truly happy. If that event never occurs, it's possible that you will never be happy with your life. You may also miss out on many opportunities along the way that could result in happiness now. Great opportunity lies in defining what a life you love consists of, designing your life to include those things, and having goals/dreams that inspire you to move forward. This means that you will enjoy the journey AND the destination once you realize the end goal or that big dream you've been working toward and finally achieved. As you pursue what brings you joy and has meaning to you, the likelihood of success, both inner and outer success, increases. Material success then adds to rather than defines your level of enjoyment of life.

How Experiencing Success Helps You Thrive

Life is all about experiences so it makes sense that if you create the experience of success for yourself as often as possible, you will thrive. You do everything you do for a reason; you get something out of it, something that is very important to you. The more you know yourself and honor yourself by ensuring that you meet your Personal Needs in ways that work throughout each and every day, the more fulfilling your life will be. Living in alignment with your Values is another important factor. If your life includes all of the things you require for success as you define it, you will thrive. You will also attract more of what you want because like attracts like. When you have more of you want – relationships, vocation, activities, possessions, experiences, etc. – you thrive. You are also much better equipped to meet life's inevitable challenges head on, from a position of strength and with resilience. You will feel fabulous and be happier, more positive, more fully alive… now that's success!

Experience Success: Key Concepts

- determine your Personal Needs and meet them in ways that work
- identify your Values and align your life with them
- define your success indicators (i.e., how you will know?)
- connect with the successes regardless of the outcome
- success can be created any time, anywhere and does not require money

Momentum Work

1. Think of something you currently do in your life that you consider yourself to be successful at. Write down your answers to the following statements relative to this:

    · The area of my life in which I feel most successful is:

    · The reasons I feel successful are:

    · What other people say about me (that I like) because of this is:

2. Identify the patterns in your life that are not creating the results you want. Write down your answers to the following statements for each of the patterns:

    · A pattern that is not working for me is:

    · What I get out of repeating this pattern (i.e., to be right, feel safe, keep the peace, feel superior, preserve my image, control, etc.) is:

    · What other people say when I get into this pattern is:

3. Identify at least 3 examples for each of the categories below. Write down your answers to the statements that follow for each example:

A) Other things I currently do and feel successful doing is:	I feel successful doing this because:	The experiences I have when doing this are:
1)	1)	1)
2)	2)	2)
3)	3)	3)
B) Something I would like to do/be is:	The reasons I want to do/be this are:	The experiences I think I would have as a result of doing/being this are:
1)	1)	1)
2)	2)	2)
3)	3)	3)
C) When I was a child I dreamed of doing/being:	The reasons I wanted to do/be this are:	The experiences I thought I would have by doing/being this are:
1)	1)	1)
2)	2)	2)
3)	3)	3)

D) Something I have felt successful doing in the past that I don't do now is:	I felt successful doing this because:	The experiences I had as a result of doing this are:
1) 2) 3)	1) 2) 3)	1) 2) 3)

4. Identify the recurring patterns in your answers to the statements on the previous pages. The ones that show up most often are your most important Personal Needs.

5. Visit http://momentumworks.com/resources.html and download "Identifying Your Personal Needs" to help you identify and clarify the patterns you revealed. Write down the needs that show up most often; these are your Personal Needs.

6. Make a list of at least 5 things you could do to meet each of your Personal Needs and incorporate activities such that you experience them every day, ideally 1 or more will be present in everything you do.

7. Go to http://momentumworks.com/resources.html and download the "Clarifying Your Values" document. Use this document to determine your 4 Core Values. Live your life in alignment with them.

Ongoing Assignment:

Design your life so that you get your Personal Needs met, live in alignment with your Values, and Experience Success throughout each day in as many ways as possible. Continue to add to your list of ways to meet your Personal Needs. Pay attention to the Needs that seem to be most important to you and focus your time and energy meeting those. Use what you know about your Personal Needs to consciously choose what you will or won't do, and to strengthen your commitment to what's most important.

Ideas About Experiencing Success:

1. Do things that come naturally/easily and you will Experience Success.

2. Consider the times in your life in which you have felt successful and why that is so.

3. Write down all of the things that you enjoy but don't think you're very good at. Do some of those things. Identify which of your Personal Needs are met in the process.

4. Create a Vision Board that includes all of the elements of a life you love and the experiences associated with it.

5. Share what you've learned about yourself with people in your life and ask them to support you in meeting your Personal Needs and creating those important experiences.

*"There is nothing either good or bad,
but thinking makes it so."*

Shakespeare

Thriving Strategy #5
Be Accepting

Be Accepting - Defined

To Be Accepting means to come to terms with your current reality, whatever that is, and move forward from there. It absolutely does not mean that you must resign yourself to being limited in any way, or settling for less than you want in life. In addition to circumstances, being accepting is also related to people, including yourself; accepting people as they are and recognizing the beauty and opportunity in that. People have a basic desire to be accepted as they are; this is a source of great struggle and discontent for many. We want ourselves, other people, circumstances, the path of our life, etc. to be different than it is or was. To Be Accepting of what is, decide what's next, and take action from there is a very powerful place to live from.

Determining Whether You Are Accepting or Settling

The best gauge of whether you are accepting or settling is your inner 'knowing', checking in with yourself as to what the truth is.   Some other useful pieces of information can be gained by deciding how important the situation in question is to you and whether or not it is something you are willing to accept.   Acceptance is not about agreeing or condoning, it is about allowing and releasing resistance. Provided your safety, boundaries, or Values are not in jeopardy, acceptance is an empowering place to approach life from. Settling comes into play when something or someone challenges these areas and you have a sense that you are settling for less than you want or need. Only YOU really know if you're settling or accepting; if you truly want to release the resistance that creates dissatisfaction it's important to tell yourself the truth about it.

The Role of Resistance on the Road to Acceptance

Resistance is a fabulous indicator of the things, people, situations, etc. that you are not currently in a place of acceptance about.   When you resist, there is potential to discover new things about yourself that can help you move to acceptance. Asking yourself questions about what you resist can generate insights that will assist you in the shift toward acceptance. Once you pinpoint the source of your resistance, you will identify the areas in which work is required to accept what is. This is true of external circumstances as well as in relationship with yourself and others. The things you resist in others (for example, they are 'selfish', 'inconsiderate', 'disorganized', etc.) are actually a reflection of characteristics about yourself that you are in resistance to or don't want to admit/look at. The more accepting you are of yourself - all of you - the more accepting you will be of others and the less resistance you will experience overall.

Some Areas in Which to Be More Accepting

People: one of the most beneficial and important areas is people. At their core people want to be accepted as they are; when you do this you give yourself the same gift. You are perfect the way you are and so is everyone else in your life. You're also 'human' and fallible and great and small and so is everyone else. When you are honest about who you are and accept all aspects of yourself, you are inherently happier and more comfortable with the real you. You will not feel the need to pretend you are someone you're not and you'll be connected to your intrinsic value. Giving yourself and the people in your life room to be who they are is something that will pay enormous dividends.

Situations: The situations in your life, particularly the ones you don't like, are another area to be more accepting of. It is in the undesirable situations that resistance comes in. "This can't be" or "how can this be?" are not statements made by someone who is in a place of acceptance. If you hear yourself saying these or similar things, it indicates that you are in resistance. When you accept things as they are, you take action from a place of strength and inclusion.

The Past: People often lament what did or didn't happen in their past. In many instances people use past experiences, events, missed opportunities, wrongdoings, etc. as a reason for why their life isn't and never will be the way they want it to be. This colors their experience of life, their happiness, their present and their future. There is nothing that can be done to change the past, so moving to a place of acceptance about it is the only way to truly get beyond it and create what you want now and into the future. If there is something required in order for you to come to closure, do that. Look for a silver lining or identify how your past has shaped who you are today. The past can be a rich learning ground when it is accepted and used as a learning opportunity.

Whatever 'is': When you dislike the way someone or something 'is', you waste a lot of energy and it is very stress producing. At times you might prefer things to be different than they are, but when you accept what is and work toward embracing it, you often discover hidden gifts. What can you learn, use, decide, choose, etc. because of how things are? Are you enriched, stronger, more compassionate, smarter, etc. as a result? What do you know that you wouldn't if things weren't as they are? Who have you met, released, learned from, helped, etc. because of your experiences? When you look for the positives in whatever 'is' in your life, you'll probably find many.

The Power in Accepting

When you accept, the power lies squarely with you. No longer are you consumed or concerned about things outside of your control; this is a very powerful place to live from. You no longer, or rarely, spend time or energy on how things are different than you want them to be and instead move to a place of 'what, if anything, am I going to do about it?'. You take charge and your energy is free for whatever action you deem necessary. Resistance melts away and you no longer use precious energy wishing things were different or being upset about the way things are. You are then engaged in more productive pursuits, focused on creating what you want, and at peace with yourself and the world around you.

Wanting Others to Change

If you're wondering "Wouldn't it be easier if someone else changed?" and you've ever attempted to change someone else, you know the short answer to this question is 'no'. On the surface it may make sense that if 'they' would change, 'you' would be happy, or at least it would be easier to accept them. In reality, what you resist about someone else is something you resist about yourself. This is where you are best served to focus your time and energy, that is to come to a place of fully accepting yourself. Whether or not the other person changes will not impact your level of happiness – in all likelihood, someone else will show up in your life (if they haven't already) with the same qualities you wanted to change in the first person. People only change if they want to change. Period. There can be great gifts in having people in your life who bring your areas of resistance to light, or act as a mirror for you. Rather than focus on how you want other people to be different, work toward acknowledging that this quality exists

79

in you and determine what you can change or accept about yourself in order to be more accepting of it. As a result, you will be more accepting of yourself and others. In the process you will be much happier with who you are and in life in general.

The Relationship Between Accepting and Standards

Accepting is about broadening your perspective and creating more space for differences, it is not about lowering standards. It centres around valuing people, situations and events in your life as they are, rather than as you think you would prefer them to be. Standards are about what you allow into your life and your personal requirements for happiness. Acceptance can be a place from which you include more people in your life by recognizing the value in who they are. Conversely, you can accept something or someone as they are and still choose not to include them in your life. In any event, acceptance does not involve lowering your standards... it is important to honor yourself in the process of acceptance.

A Framework for Acceptance

Coming from the framework that everyone does their best at all times can be very helpful in the area of acceptance. Another important consideration is that someone's best can look different on a given day or in a given moment. Remembering that you are the only person you have any capacity to control may also help. When you approach the world with these things in mind, acceptance occurs more readily.

Acceptance = Flow   Resistance = Struggle

Life is not meant to be a struggle, yet so many people operate from that place. Struggle doesn't lead to happiness. When you remember that everyone, including you, is doing their best and that you cannot control anyone or anything outside of yourself, you are reminded that in any given moment you can change how you hold a specific event or person in your life. If you are resistant to something, you have full control over your thoughts and actions such that you move to accept. Resistance is a losing battle – it leads to struggle and robs you of energy, flow, joy and power. Acceptance, on the other hand, creates energy, flow, joy and power. The choice is yours.

'Agree to Disagree' as a Strategy for Acceptance

Agree to disagree is a concept based on acknowledging and respecting that others have a right to their own opinions/beliefs and that it's not necessary that they be in alignment with yours. Rather than attempt to get someone to change their opinion and agree with you, you can agree to disagree. Everyone is entitled to their opinions… they are neither 'right' nor 'wrong'; they are merely different. Given that everyone comes together with a different set of life experiences, it stands to reason that not everyone will agree with you. Your experiences are what lead to your opinions and beliefs, this is the same for everyone. Whether or not your opinions/beliefs contribute to or detract from your quality of life is up to you to decide; the same is true for the people in your life. Many arguments and much stress can be avoided by employing this strategy. By allowing people to have their own opinions/beliefs, you will succeed in increasing your level of acceptance and the quality of your relationships.

How Being Accepting Helps You Thrive

At a very basic level, everyone wants to be accepted as they are. By Being Accepting, you lead by example and in the process enhance your self-esteem. The more you accept yourself, the more you accept others and the happier you are. From an energetic perspective, acceptance is energy producing... it fuels many of the positive outcomes in your life. You are in charge and empowered rather than at the mercy of the people and events in your life; you feel good about you, others and your world. You leave room for mistakes, let go of the past, release the need for perfection, and allow everyone and everything to be as is... including you. From this place you are in a position to take action in a way that is empowering, honoring and effective. You live in the present and come to terms with things in the present moment, seeing the value and opportunity that lies in your current reality. You feel empowered to take action in the direction of what you want, and that's what you're here for; this leads to fulfillment and helps you to thrive.

Be Accepting: Key Concepts

- everyone wants to be accepted as they are; accept yourself and others
- acceptance = flow, resistance = struggle
- you cannot control anything or anyone but yourself
- resistance is a mirror for things you don't accept about yourself

Momentum Work

1. Identify your main areas of resistance by answering the following statements thoroughly:

The Top 3 areas of resistance in my life are:	The reasons for my resistance are:
The person in my life that I have the most issues with is:	The major issues are:
The event that has most negatively affected my life is:	The reasons it has negatively affected my life are:
I get most upset when people:	I find this upsetting because:

2. Choose 1 of your Top 3 areas of resistance to move toward acceptance in.

- Identify the prices you pay as a result of being in resistance in this area
- List the gains (i.e., to be right, feel superior, feel powerful, avoid effort, stay in your comfort zone, protect your self-image, meet your Personal Needs, etc.) you get from being in resistance in this area
- Identify the qualities in yourself that you are resisting in this area

3. Take steps to Be Accepting.

- Create a list of at least 5 beneficial ways for you to realize the gains you identified above
- Write down at least 3 things that will help you be more positive about each of the qualities you are resisting about yourself in this area
- Write a paragraph (at least 150 words) describing how your life will improve as a result of being accepting in this area.

Ongoing Assignment

Be conscious of your areas of resistance and curious about their origin. Identify what it is about you that the resistance occurs. Connect with the bigger 'game' you are playing (acceptance) and how it will help you move closer to what's most important to you. Remember that everyone is always doing their best, including you.

Ideas About Being Accepting

1. Find a place of compassion from which to approach people/ situations you resist

2. Keep an Acceptance Journal and include:

   - what you resist
   - why you resist it
   - how it is a mirror for you
   - prices you pay for resisting it
   - gains you experience by resisting it
   - whether or not it is in your best interest to be accepting of it
   - ways to move to acceptance (provided it's in your best interest)
   - how you can look at it from a different, more positive, compassionate perspective

3. The people with whom and situations in which you are most likely to give up what you want in order to be accepted provide valuable insights into what you resist about yourself

4. When you have a resistant thought, replace it with an accepting one

5. Identify the value in the characteristics you resist in others

6. Use your level of acceptance of others as a gauge for your level of self-acceptance; take action as required to accept fully

7. If you find yourself struggling, ask yourself "What am I resisting?"

8. Find the value, joy and humor in 'what is'

*"When we truly care for ourselves,
it becomes possible to care far more profoundly
about other people."*

Eda LeShan

Thriving Strategy #6
Practice Selfness

Selfness - Defined

Selfness is fundamentally about putting yourself first. It means making sure that your needs are taken care of before you turn your attention to others. Think of the emergency instructions given on an airplane "… in the event of an emergency, place your oxygen mask on first and then assist the other person". There is a reason you are given these instructions; if you aren't breathing, you won't be in a position to help anyone else. Practicing Selfness will contribute significantly to your likelihood of thriving. It is not a 'selfish' act. Thinking about it in other than selfish terms might contradict many of the things you learned about generosity, kindness, thoughtfulness, etc. The key is that you practice these and other 'niceties' on yourself first and by doing that you will naturally have more to give to others. You will also come from a place of abundance rather than lack. This means when you give to others it will be from a willing, open place as opposed to an obligatory, potentially resentful place. If you're not taking care of yourself, you'll be of little help to anyone else. The essence of Selfness is caring for yourself and treating yourself like the most important person in your life… because you are.

Selfness vs. Selfishness

In order to truly understand the concept of Selfness, it is important to distinguish it from selfishness. Selfness centres around caring for yourself first so that you thrive and are in a place of abundance when giving to others. Selfishness, on the other hand, centres around doing for yourself with little or no regard for others. Selfishness often stems from a sense of lack. The belief that 'there is not enough for everyone, so I'm going to get mine before you get yours' is common in the realm of selfishness. It is a win-lose proposition. When you practice Selfness, you care for yourself in such a way that you have time, energy and reserves for the important people, activities and other things in your life. By making Selfness a high priority, you will actually accomplish more because you will be taking the time to relax, recharge and renew your energy in all areas of your life.

Balancing Selfness and Responsibilities

There's no doubt about it, responsibilities can put a monkey wrench in the best laid plans if you allow them to. It can be a challenge to put yourself first amid the many demands on your time, but it is imperative if you want to thrive. It may serve you well to remind yourself that Practicing Selfness leads to achieving more and enjoying your achievements more. Evaluating the multitude of responsibilities you have taken on with an eye toward reducing them is another valuable exercise. At the end of the day, it all boils down to deciding what's most important and determining what you will let go of in order to set yourself up for success. Chances are that you have some obligations on your list that you can rid yourself of, some tasks that you can consolidate or outsource, or some activities to eliminate that are not very important; all of which can free up time for you. You will probably discover a number of time wasters to eliminate as well. Once you determine what you actually spend time doing, you will be in a position to evaluate your situation and decide what will stay and what will go so that you have more time to Practice Selfness.

Successfully Practice Selfness Despite Past Results

Persistence in the pursuit of what's most important to you is a key element of success. Thomas Edison tried 10,000+ ways to create a light bulb before he actually succeeded. It's unlikely that it will take you 10,000 attempts to commit to Practicing Selfness, but past 'failures' are not a valid reason to give up on this very important aspect of living a life you love. Past history can be a useful source of information as to why you have not realized long term success in this area to date; that's where its usefulness ends. Consider the personal, environmental and foundational factors that have contributed to your results thus far and use this information to help set yourself up for success now. Your past holds valuable information that will lead to your ultimate success. If you approach it as an experiment rather than seeking 'the' solution, you'll come to realize that the road to success often involves detours and you'll enjoy the experience more. There can be as much value in knowing what doesn't work as there is in knowing what does. Connecting your actions to your Personal Needs and Values, as identified in Chapter 4, will solidify your connection with and commitment to Practicing Selfness. This holds true for all areas of your life and any goal that you have. The key is to connect to the benefits in as many ways and on as many levels as possible and stay the course. Rather than give up when you get off course, make a correction and keep going.

The Relationship Between an Interesting Life and Practicing Selfness

By having an interesting life, you will spend your time and energy focused on you rather than on what others are doing or not doing. When your life is filled with fun and interesting things, you have more than enough positive, inspiring and energizing things to talk about. When you are excited about and fully engaged in living your best life, you are less likely to pass judgment on others, gossip, be envious, or engage in other counterproductive activities or emotions. If you find yourself engaged in any of these or similar counterproductive things, use them as indicators that your life is not interesting enough and turn your attention back to Selfness and building a more interesting life. As a result, you will feel better about yourself and have more time to Practice Selfness. By virtue of living an interesting life, you will incorporate things that lead to an optimal experience of life. You will also have a more positive outlook, healthier relationships, and more self-respect. An interesting life generally includes fun, learning, growing, interacting, connecting and relaxing... in varying degrees depending on the individual. It will result in having more of what you want and a life well loved.

Releasing Guilt Associated with Practicing Selfness

Even though it may seem as though other people 'trigger' it, guilt, like every emotion, is self-generated. People generally feel guilt when, for whatever reason, they think they have done something wrong, don't deserve more, or do something that is contrary to who they believe they are. Guilt is a way to get back at yourself when any of these or similar conditions exist. Guilt keeps you from realizing your full potential and accepting yourself completely; it generally indicates a state of denial and serves no constructive purpose. You may feel better in the moment, justify an action or inaction, or deny the truth about something in the short term, but long term it will not help you thrive. It is possible that guilt will come up as you begin to Practice Selfness, or perhaps even at the mere thought of it. If this is the case, you have beliefs about what putting yourself first says about you that may prevent you from actually doing it. It probably goes against what you have learned or believe about doing for others vs. doing for yourself, generosity, kindness, thoughtfulness, or any number of other things. Becoming clear about the source of your guilt and the beliefs that support it, then coming up with new beliefs

93

that will support you to Practice Selfness, is a useful exercise in working through and getting beyond guilt. Knowing and understanding this goes a long way toward helping you let go of guilt and doing what is best for you.

If People Think You're Being Selfish

It is possible that other people will consider your practice of Selfness to be selfish. Whenever you make changes that affect people in your life, it opens up the possibility that they might not be as enthusiastic about the changes as you are. Many people equate putting yourself first with being selfish because they have learned, potentially from many different sources throughout their lives, that this is so. It requires a shift in thinking and beliefs to get to a place of knowing that there is a difference between Selfness and selfishness. It requires a strong commitment and sense of self to Practice Selfness and feel good about it, rather than worry about what others might think. One great way to do this is to connect with the benefits of Practicing Selfness and keep them at the top of your mind. Whenever someone in your life calls it into question, remind yourself of the benefits and continue on your path. Another strategy is to connect with the results you are creating by making the choice to put yourself first. By Practicing Selfness, you will set a good example for people in your life, even if they (or you) don't see it at first. Find out if they are interested in understanding it more and if so, share what you have learned. Invite them along on your journey. Sometimes the changes you make in yourself stir up fear in those who are used to you being a certain way. When you include them, it can alleviate their fears and put them in a position to support the changes you are committed to make. At the end of the day, Practicing Selfness is about you doing what is best for you and believing that you deserve it. Once you reach that place, you will cease to be concerned with what other people think.

Practicing Selfness and Relationships

While it is true that some people may not like the changes you make around the practice of Selfness, it is more likely that the important people in your life will support your decision, especially if you share what you're doing and why. People who really care about you and want the best for you will probably be happy to see you taking better care of yourself. What may at first appear to be something that has you spending less time being with and doing for others, generally becomes a way to enhance the quality of your relationships. When you come to a relationship with your tank overflowing, as opposed to running on empty, you bring more of yourself to every interaction. You enter from a place of abundance and as a result, you give to others from a place of having more than enough. This enables you to give from a place of generosity without taking anything from yourself; it is the difference between desire and obligation. When you have enough time, energy, health, wealth, etc. to thrive, you will have more of yourself to give to others – and you'll feel great doing it!

The Relationship Between Communication and Selfness

Open, honest communication is an important component of Practicing Selfness. It involves honoring yourself by being honest about your thoughts, feelings, opinions and desires. This applies equally to when things are the way you want them to be as when they're not. It means being honest about what is working and what is not. It is much easier to be open and honest when things are going well, when you are happy, in agreement, getting what you want, etc. The challenge arises in sharing the things you aren't as pleased about. Fears of losing a relationship, causing damage to a relationship, or appearing in a less than favorable light can be significant deterrents to having an open, honest conversation. The primary purpose of Practicing Selfness is to honor and take care of yourself first. Pretending that things are fine when they are not does not serve this purpose. Nor does talking yourself out of the importance of something in order to avoid addressing it, or avoiding 'tough' conversations. It is of paramount importance to equip yourself with the tools you need to communicate openly and honestly in a constructive way that enhances the quality of your relationships. By doing this you'll increase your confidence and self-esteem while honoring yourself and others in the process.

How Practicing Selfness Helps You Thrive

The very act of Practicing Selfness helps you make great strides toward thriving. It requires that you get beyond worrying about what other people think and do what's best for you. In order to do this, you will have come to realize that you are not only worth taking care of, you are deserving of it. In the process you will boost your self-confidence and self-esteem and attract more of the people and situations you desire and require to live a life you love. You will also know that helping others from a place of abundance is more honoring to you and them. You will have everything you need every day and you will be living your life in a way that you experience success throughout each day. Your outlook will be positive, you will have reserves to help you through challenging times, and you will experience less stress. You will have more time and energy for the things that are most important and you'll say 'no' to what's not important to you. You will spend more time in the flow of life rather than struggling through the days. You will engage in things you are passionate about, nurture relationships in meaningful ways, and experience more joy in your life. Practicing Selfness is imperative if you want to truly thrive.

Practice Selfness: Key Concepts

- take care of yourself first
- abundance leads to higher quality giving
- make your life very interesting
- Selfness enhances relationships

Momentum Work

1. Create a list of 15 things that you could do to Practice Selfness; be sure to include at least 10 things you could do on your own and include all open, honest conversation opportunities as well.

   • Identify the 3 Selfness activities that are most appealing to you

2. Refer to the prioritized list you created in Chapter 3 (Include Play) #2 of the ways you spend your time:

   a. choose one Priority 3 item that you will eliminate

   b. identify one activity from your Top 3 Selfness activities list that you will do this week (1 hour or more)

3. Choose one open, honest conversation that you will have in the spirit of improving an important relationship. Visit http://momentumworks.com/resources.html and download the Framework for Effective Communication and use it as a guide for this conversation. Have the conversation within 3 days.

4. Choose one activity that you have not done before from your Practice Selfness list and do it within 10 days.

Ongoing Assignment

Practice Selfness for the remainder of the time you are working through this book (and beyond if you really want to thrive). Add 30 minutes per week until you spend at least 2 hours each week Practicing Selfness. Increase as required for you to thrive.

Ideas About Practicing Selfness:

1. Continue to add to your list of ways to Practice Selfness, here are some ideas:

   - Get at least 8 hours (or the optimal amount of time for you) of sleep each night
   - Go to a movie (the kind you like best)
   - Meditate
   - Visit a market (food or other) that interests you
   - Do yoga, pilates or other mind-body-spirit activity
   - Spend some time at a favorite book store
   - Buy yourself that new tool you've had your eye on
   - Visit an art supply store and discover ways to express yourself creatively
   - Visit an art gallery
   - Treat yourself to a spa day (at home or at a favorite spa)

- Take a walk through a beautiful park and notice which plants/flowers you prefer
- Write in a journal
- Visit a winery and do some tastings
- Take a bubble bath; light candles and include your favorite essential oil
- Visit a glass blowing gallery or specialty store
- Enroll in an art, martial arts, or other appealing class
- Browse at a fabulous gift shop or tool store
- Buy yourself some flowers
- Have lunch or breakfast at a restaurant with an appealing setting
- Go for a drive without a specific destination… follow your intuition and stop wherever it tells you to along the way
- Read
- Go for a walk anywhere that strikes you and be very mindful of the beauty around you
- Try something you've never done before
- Play
- Spend quality time with important people
- Say 'no' when you mean it
- Clear the air with people in your life as required
- Tell people what you appreciate about them
- Say thank you often

2. Each day that you Practice Selfness, write down all of the benefits you experienced by doing so. Continue doing this until the benefits are top of mind and Selfness is an integral part of your life.

3. Ask yourself the question "What would I say to/do for my best friend in this situation?" often. Say or do that to/for yourself.

4. Check-in with yourself daily about how you feel physically, mentally and emotionally; course correct as necessary to thrive.

5. Be open, honest and respectful in your conversations.

6. Pay attention to your thoughts and replace self-defeating/diminishing thoughts with empowering/supportive ones.

*"Go confidently in the direction of your dreams.
Live the life you've imagined."*

Henry David Thoreau

Thriving Strategy #7
Maintain Momentum

Maintain Momentum - Defined

Maintain Momentum means to keep the energy going around creating what's most important to you. It is also about maintaining momentum around the work you have done in your life as a result of reading and completing this book. It involves continuing to thrive by keeping what you've learned alive and remaining in the process of incorporating it more and more as you move forward. It requires conscious action and application in your daily life and doing whatever is necessary to ensure that you stay the course. As a result of reading this book, completing the assignments, and making certain adjustments you are probably enjoying life a lot more than when you started this journey. You have likely created some momentum in your life around the things that you have determined to be most important to you. Much like a snowball picks up energy and velocity and gets bigger as it rolls down a hill, you have started to build your own snowball and the effort required to continue to build it will be reduced over time. It is easier to maintain or accelerate momentum than it is to build it over and over again. The beauty of momentum is that at some point it takes on an energy of its own, which means that creating great results takes less effort. By maintaining the momentum you have created, you will accelerate your progress and enjoy better results more quickly with less effort. You have likely experienced this phenomenon at some point in your life. Life is about enjoying the journey, not about struggle... momentum plays an important role in helping you enjoy the journey.

The Importance of Maintaining Momentum

The importance of Maintaining Momentum cannot be overstated. Not only will you get where you are going faster and with less effort, you will also reduce your likelihood of reverting back to life as you used to live it. As mentioned previously, once momentum is going it is much easier to maintain and even accelerate, than it is to start over. It takes time to solidify the changes you are making and create roots that will generate long term results. It takes time for new ways of being and doing to become second nature and form a new norm for how you live your life. By Maintaining Momentum, you will continue to move forward in creating the life that is best for you and enjoy the life you are living along the way more. Leveraging the energy of momentum helps to accelerate progress, which acts as fuel to inspire and motivate you to continue on the path you have started to pave for yourself. You will continue to reap the benefits of making choices that are best for you, increase your self-esteem and confidence, and enhance your relationships. You will experience success regularly and feel great about yourself and your life.

The Role Others Play in Maintaining Momentum

Other people can play an important role in Maintaining Momentum so it is important to include them. If you truly want to create a foundation for your life that ensures you will thrive, including people who want the best for you and will support you in the process is imperative. Similar to momentum, other people add their energy to what you want and help you get where you're going more quickly and easily. It is important to be selective when choosing your support team; make sure you include people who will add to rather than detract from your efforts. You will be best served to include people who will cheer you on, believe in you, and not buy into your reasons or excuses no matter how logical or valid they seem. If you feel energized after an interaction with someone, they are a good candidate for your team. Naysayers, energy drains, and negative people are best excluded. If you feel exhausted or have less energy after an interaction with someone, they are not the right person to include on your team. If you've ever had 'buddies' to help you reach a goal - i.e., a workout partner, a Coach, a team you played on, an accountability group such as for a diet, or a mastermind group for business or personal goals - you will have first-hand experience of the value of including others to Maintain Momentum and focus. They can also fortify your resolve on those days that you'd rather not do what you said was important. If you let other people know where you're headed, you will stay on track more often and you'll get back on track faster when you inevitably veer off. They will remind you of your destination and alert you when you're off course. Chances are, you'll enjoy the journey more as well.

How This Book Can Help You Maintain Momentum

The body of work you have just completed, and hopefully will continue to incorporate, is designed to help you generate long lasting results. In essence it is designed to help you Maintain Momentum. By Taking Charge of your life, you will be taking action around what's most important to you from a powerful, solution-oriented place. Being Grateful will help you feel terrific about your life and all that you have to appreciate. You will also attract more of what you want because you get what you focus on. By Including Play you will experience more passion, inspiration, fun and joy, all of which are cleaner fuels for living life and loving it. Designing your life so that you Experience Success in all that you do will enhance your overall experience of life, the quality of your relationships (with yourself and others) and your ease of movement toward what you want most. By Being Accepting, your relationship with yourself and the reality of the people and situations in your life will be more harmonious, you will experience less resistance and therefore have a smoother journey. Practicing Selfness will ensure that you are taking care of yourself to the extent that you have an abundance of what you need to thrive. This means you'll have more energy and reserves to put toward creating your best life. Including other people in your journey will help you keep what is important to you at the top of your mind and get you back on course when you go off. All of this will contribute greatly to maintaining the momentum you have created and living a life you love.

How Maintaining Momentum Helps You Thrive

When you create momentum and maintain it, it tends to take on an energy of its own and helps you get where you are going more quickly and easily. This means that you will be creating and enjoying more of the things you really want with more ease and frequency. When you are making noticeable progress, you will feel better about yourself and your life and you will be inspired to keep going. As you fill your life with more and more of the elements of a life you love, you will have more energy and you will experience more fun, joy and passion. In the process, you will be including important people in meaningful ways and enjoying richer, higher quality relationships. As you have more of what you want, you will attract more of what you want. You will be happier, more positive, and more magnetic to the elements of your best life. The energy of momentum will carry you through life in flow rather than resistance and it will fuel your desire to continue on the journey you have started. As you experience the many benefits of momentum, your commitment to yourself and to continuing this journey will be cemented. Over time, the Thriving Strategies can become a way of life that is very natural, easy and empowering. Maintaining Momentum is a key component of thriving in all areas of your life.

Maintain Momentum: Key Concepts

- get what you want more quickly with less effort
- live in a state of flow more often
- include others in the process
- important for long term integration

Momentum Work

1. Create a list of at least 10 ways that you could Maintain Momentum in your life:

    - Choose one that you will implement on an ongoing basis and start doing it within the next 4 days.

2. Refer back to the various lists you have created in past assignments and identify which of your Personal Needs and Values are/would be met through each item on your list.

3. Write a paragraph (at least 150 words) to describe how you imagine things will be different (how you will be feeling differently, what you will be doing differently, and what will be happening differently) with momentum at work in your life.

4. Create a support group of at least 3 other people who will help you stay on course, maintain the momentum you have created, and thrive. Develop an accountability structure with regular check-ins and course correct as required.

Ongoing Assignment

Refer to the Ongoing Assignments in each Chapter and set aside a minimum of 2 hours per week to continue working on those that you believe are most beneficial. Ideally, you will continue with all of them in varying amounts and at different times. Continue to acknowledge your progress and wins along the way through rewards, celebrations and anything else that works well for you.

Ideas About Maintaining Momentum:

1. Implement a 'buddy' system where you check-in with someone on a regular (at least bi-weekly) basis with progress, challenges and to celebrate wins

2. Include other people in things that you have tended to neglect in the past (i.e., exercise, diet, paperwork, projects, etc.)

3. Connect your Personal Needs and Values to everything you do so that you have a greater connection to and purpose for what you are doing

4. Follow your intuition about what you commit to; if it doesn't feel right, say 'no'

5. Delegate pieces of projects to people who enjoy them and are good at them; it will be a win-win and you will get better quality results more quickly, easily and enjoyably

6. Create 'mastermind' groups around larger goals and projects and include people who have skills and attributes that will contribute to the results you want to create

Michelle Richardson

"Greatness is a road leading towards the unknown."

Charles de Gaulle

Resources

Michelle Richardson has designed and will continue to develop resources that will assist you in your ongoing journey. Some of these include:

Momentum Works Inc.

http://MomentumWorks.com
This is Michelle's coaching website; it offers various opportunities, events and other resources (many of which are free) designed to help you thrive in all areas of your life. As with any website, it is in a continuous state of evolution.

Coaching Program: From Surviving to Thriving in 30 Days

Michelle coaches groups and individuals through her book over a 30 day period to help them make significant progress quickly. Available via TeleClass or in person. Email info@momentumworks.com for more details.

Companion Workbook

The Companion Workbook contains all of the assignments, exercises and assessments from this book in one place. By using the Companion Workbook, you will have all of your 'best life' elements in one place for easy reference. Available in electronic format at http://MomentumWorks.com for $4.99.

Go From Surviving To Thriving

http://GoFromSurvivingToThriving.com
This website will be specifically designed for people on the path from surviving to thriving. There will be resources, ideas, online groups, a buddy system, a blog, and other resources designed to help you stay connected and remain in the process of thriving and living a life you love.

Absolutely Fabulous You

http://AbsolutelyFabulousYou.com
This is a website that will be developed to celebrate and support your greatness. It will include resources, ideas, online groups, a buddy system, a blog, and other resources designed to help you discover and celebrate Absolutely Fabulous YOU!

Absolutely Fabulous U

http://AbsolutelyFabulousU.com
This website will be designed for people who want to take on a leading role in celebrating and supporting the greatness of others. It will be an online 'university' of sorts where Coaches, Managers, Entrepreneurs, Teachers, and other professionals will have an opportunity to be trained and certified to lead the various programs that Michelle has developed.

Over time, more resources will be available to help you, while helping Michelle realize her vision to have a profoundly positive impact in the world and manifest her Life's Calling: To Evoke Greatness on a Global Scale.

A Fitting Tale

You may have read this, or some variation of it, at some point... given the nature of my book, I thought it fitting to include it here...

When things in your life seem almost too much to handle, when 24 hours in a day are not enough, remember the mayonnaise jar and 2 cups of coffee.

A professor stood before his philosophy class and had some items in front of him. When the class began, wordlessly, he picked up a very large and empty mayonnaise jar and proceeded to fill it with golf balls.

He then asked the students if the jar was full. They agreed that it was.

The professor then picked up a box of pebbles and poured them into the jar. He shook the jar lightly. The pebbles rolled into the open areas between the golf balls.

He then asked the students again if the jar was full. They agreed it was.

The professor next picked up a box of sand and poured it into the jar. Of course, the sand filled up everything else.

He asked once more if the jar was full. The students responded with a unanimous "yes".

The professor then produced two cups of coffee from under the table and poured the entire contents into the jar, effectively filling the empty space between the sand. The students laughed.

"Now," said the professor, as the laughter subsided, "I want you to recognize that this jar represents your life.

"The golf balls are the important things - family, children, health, friends, spirituality and favorite passions - things that if everything else was lost and only they remained, your life would still be full.

"The pebbles are the other things that matter like your job, house and car.

"The sand is everything else – the small stuff."

"If you put the sand into the jar first" he continued, "there is no room for the pebbles or the golf balls. The same goes for life. If you spend all of your time and energy on the small stuff, you will never have room for the things that are important to you."

"So... pay attention to the things that are critical to your happiness. Play with your children. Take time to get medical checkups. Take your significant other out for dinner. Play another 18. There will always be time to clean the house and fix the disposal."

"Take care of the golf balls first – the things that really matter. Set your priorities. The rest is just sand."

One of the students raised her hand and inquired what the coffee represented.

The professor smiled. "I'm glad you asked. It just goes to show you that no matter how full your life may seem, there's always room for a cup of coffee with a friend."

- Source Unknown

Mind what matters...

Michelle

"To move the world we must first move ourselves."

Socrates

About the Author

Michelle Richardson, IAC-CC

Since founding Momentum Works Inc. in 2001, Michelle has coached thousands of people including entrepreneurs, managers, individuals, groups and teams. A former Instructor for CoachVille and one of a select group of IAC Certified Coaches worldwide, Michelle has demonstrated highly successful leadership in the professional world, in the community and among her peers. She is passionate about working with people to support their success professionally and personally. Her highly successful business background includes Microsoft and SuperPages; add this to her unique blend of training and life experience and it's a winning combination.

Michelle's Vision is to have a profoundly positive impact in the world and, as evidenced by a nomination for the YWCA of Vancouver Women of Distinction Award, she is doing just that. Called to Evoke Greatness on a Global Scale, she makes progress toward this through her relationships, coaching practice, programs, seminars, workshops, TeleClasses, Inspirational Tips and now, this book.

Michelle lives in the Lower Mainland of beautiful British Columbia. She loves to spend time with her family & friends, travel and go play outside. Also an accomplished athlete, whatever Michelle does, she plays to win.

Learn more at: http://MomentumWorks.com

CPSIA information can be obtained
at www.ICGtesting.com
Printed in the USA
LVOW10s0007111117
555851LV00008B/54/P